31.00

EXPLORING THE
PERSIAN EMPIRE

by Peggy Caravantes

12 STORY LIBRARY

www.12StoryLibrary.com

Copyright © 2018 by 12-Story Library, Mankato, MN 56003. All rights reserved. No part of this book may be reproduced or utilized in any form or by any means without written permission from the publisher.

12-Story Library is an imprint of Bookstaves and Press Room Editions

Produced for 12-Story Library by Red Line Editorial

Photographs ©: Aleksandar Todorovic/Shutterstock Images, cover, 1; bogdanserban/iStockphoto, 4; David Holt London CC2.0 (https://www.flickr.com/photos/zongo/), 5; Gerry Embleton/North Wind Picture Archives, 6; A. Davey CC2.0, 7; North Wind Picture Archives, 8, 13, 22, 25; Borna_Mirahmadian/Shutterstock Images, 9, 14; tunart/iStockphoto, 10, 28; Kathleen Tyler Conklin CC2.0 (www.flickr.com/photos/ktylerconk/), 11; IgorSPb/iStockphoto, 12; Pavliha/iStockphoto, 15; duncan1890/iStockphoto, 17, 23; milosk50/Shutterstock Images, 18; Xuan Che CC2.0, 19; OPIS Zagreb/Shutterstock Images, 20; Claudiovidri/Shutterstock Images, 24, 29; AP Images, 27; Ninara CC2.0, 26

Content Consultant: John Hyland, Associate Professor of History, Christopher Newport University

Library of Congress Cataloging-in-Publication Data
Names: Caravantes, Peggy, 1935- author.
Title: Exploring the Persian Empire / by Peggy Caravantes.
Other titles: Exploring ancient civilizations (12 Story Library (Firm))
Description: Mankato, MN : 12 Story Library, 2018. | Series: Exploring
   ancient civilizations | Includes bibliographical references and index.
Identifiers: LCCN 2016047648 (print) | LCCN 2016057744 (ebook) | ISBN
   9781632354686 (hardcover : alk. paper) | ISBN 9781632355331 (pbk. : alk.
   paper) | ISBN 9781621435853 (hosted e-book)
Subjects: LCSH: Iran--History--To 640--Juvenile literature.
Classification: LCC DS281 .C37 2018 (print) | LCC DS281 (ebook) | DDC
   935/.705--dc23
LC record available at https://lccn.loc.gov/2016047648

Printed in the United States of America
022017

Access free, up-to-date content on this topic plus a full digital version of this book. Scan the QR code on page 31 or use your school's login at 12StoryLibrary.com.

Table of Contents

1
King Cyrus Was the First Great Ruler

The Persian Empire was made up of all of Iran and much of today's other Middle Eastern countries. The empire existed from 550 BCE to 330 BCE. It was one of the greatest powers in the world at that time. At its height, it was the largest empire the world had ever known.

The ancient Persians had been nomads for many years. By the 600s BCE, they settled in the southern part of what is now Iran. A man named Cyrus was a leader from the Achaemenid dynasty. He led a war against the Medes in 550 BCE. He took over Media, which is now northern Iran. He also conquered Lydia in western Turkey and Babylon in Iraq. He is called Cyrus the Great.

Stories tell us that Cyrus the Great was different from many other ancient conquerors. Ancient writers

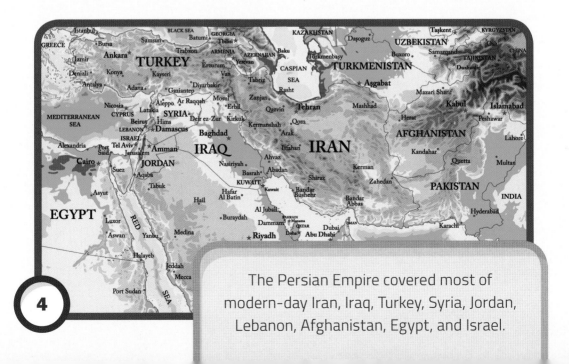

The Persian Empire covered most of modern-day Iran, Iraq, Turkey, Syria, Jordan, Lebanon, Afghanistan, Egypt, and Israel.

THE CYRUS CYLINDER

Most of the information about Cyrus comes from outsiders such as the Greek Herodotus. There are few sources that let the Persians speak for themselves. But one is the Cyrus Cylinder. In 539 BCE, Cyrus invaded Babylon. At the time, most royal messages were written on clay cylinders. So Cyrus ordered the scribes of Babylon to write a description of his greatness on a cylinder, too. Most historians agree that the text on the cylinder is not completely accurate. Much of it is likely propaganda, or false praise.

The Cyrus Cylinder is on display at the British Museum.

such as the Greek author Herodotus used him as an example of an ideal ruler. They say he cooperated with the people he conquered. As long as people paid tribute to Persia, they could have their own customs and religion. Cyrus's acceptance of other cultures paved the way for the Persian Empire to reach new heights.

2.12 million

Approximate size, in square miles (5.5 million sq km), of the Persian Empire.

- The ancient Persian Empire was the greatest power of its time.
- A leader called Cyrus the Great conquered many regions.
- Cyrus tolerated other cultures to gain the cooperation of conquered people.

Clever Battle Plans Helped the Empire Grow

King Cyrus expanded the Persian Empire victory after victory. Herodotus tells a story about Cyrus's conquest of Lydia, which happened sometime between 545 and 540 BCE. Cyrus had a clever plan to defeat King Croesus of Lydia, the richest man in the world. Cyrus put his men on camels and put them in front. The Lydian horses did not like the camels' strange odor when the two armies met. The enemies' horses bolted. The Persians won the battle.

Cyrus and his army approached Babylon in 539 BCE. At the time, it was the largest city in the world and an important cultural and religious center. Cyrus decided not to use force to take over the city. Instead he took advantage of the people's dislike for their king Nabonidus. He had failed to observe religious ceremonies and had been careless with religious icons. Cyrus restored them to the people. His actions allowed him to claim himself ruler

Cyrus convinced the Babylonians that King Nabonidus spent too much time worshipping the moon instead of honoring the gods.

over Babylon. This victory increased the Persian Empire to an area around two million square miles (5.5 million sq km) in size.

King Cyrus's son Cambyses took over the empire when Cyrus died in 530 BCE. Cambyses set his sights on conquering Egypt. He had a little help with his battle plans, though. Cambyses received advice from a man named Phanes, who happened to be a Greek general in the Egyptian army. Cambyses successfully defeated the Egyptians in 525 BCE. But Cambyses would not rule for long. He died mysteriously in 522 BCE, after ruling for just seven years.

51
Minimum age at which Cyrus the Great died in battle, fighting nomads in central Asia.

- Cyrus may have used camel odor to defeat King Croesus.
- Cyrus had a different plan to win the city of Babylon.
- The unpopularity of King Nabonidus meant Cyrus had an easy time convincing Babylonians he would be a better ruler.
- Cyrus's son Cambyses took over Egypt.

The tomb of King Cyrus is located in Pasargadae in modern-day Iran.

Darius I Organized the Empire

Darius I was a relative of Cyrus. He was in his late twenties in 522 BCE when he came to power. The Persian Empire he ruled covered a vast amount of land. People of many cultures lived there. Darius realized the empire had to have more organization. He divided the land into 20 tax districts. These were called satrapies.

A governor, or satrap, ruled over each district. Satraps reported directly to the king. They were responsible for collecting the annual tributes to the king. Tributes varied from required military service to taxes on goods and travel. From time to time, Darius sent out a group of trusted men to check on the income and spending of the satraps. These royal inspectors acted as the eyes and ears of the king.

Map of the empire under Darius I with the different satrapies

PERSIAN EMPIRE
Under Darius, About 500 B.C.
with principal Satrapies.

SCALE OF MILES
0   100   200   300   400

The Persian Empire
Grecian Territory
Royal road from Susa to Sardis

Darius built a palace at Persepolis to store tributes.

Some of the larger satrapies were divided. There were governors for each of the smaller areas that were probably approved by the king.

19

Number of battles Darius and his generals won in one year to secure his power.

- Darius organized the empire into 20 satrapies.
- Each satrapy was headed by a satrap, who collected annual tributes for the king.
- Darius sent military commanders to keep the satrapies from growing too powerful.

But Darius did not want the satraps to have too much power. He sent military commanders to inspect all the satrapies. They reported directly to the king.

Darius used the money and labor from the tributes to build new roads and water supplies. Under Darius, the empire became organized and efficient.

THINK ABOUT IT

Why did Darius not want the satraps to have too much power? Are there any similarities to the U.S. government?

4

A Network of Roads Made Good Connections

The large size of the Persian Empire required a good way to communicate and to collect taxes. Darius realized early on that information was the key to controlling the lands. Messages between cities needed to arrive quickly and safely.

The Greek writer Herodotus describes the Persians' system of roads. According to Herodotus, the Persians figured out how far a horse could travel in one day without becoming too tired. Along each road, stations were built one day's ride apart. Each messenger rode approximately 19 miles (30 km). Stations had fresh horses and grooms to care for them. A man at each station made sure a message passed from one rider to the next. The most famous

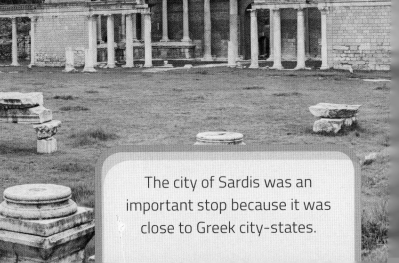

The city of Sardis was an important stop because it was close to Greek city-states.

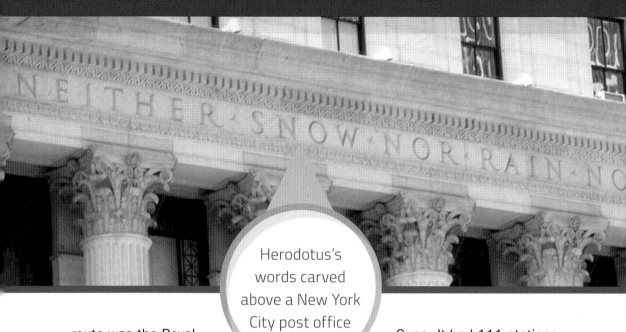

Herodotus's words carved above a New York City post office

route was the Royal Road. A 1,600-mile (2,600-km) section connected Sardis, the capital of Lydia, to the Persian capital at Susa. It had 111 stations to provide food and shelter to travelers. Day and night, even in bad weather, the king could be in touch with his empire.

UNITED STATES POSTAL SERVICE MOTTO

Many people think the United States Postal Service has a motto. It does not have an official one, but the following words were carved above the entrance of a New York City post office. "Neither snow nor rain nor heat nor gloom of night stays these couriers from the swift completion of their appointed rounds." These words actually come from Herodotus's description of the Persian couriers.

12

Number of days it took for a message to travel from Sardis to Susa.

- The size of the Persian Empire required a good communication system.
- Stations were built one day's ride apart along all the roads.
- The Royal Road was the most famous.
- Security was tight for messages sent on the roads.

The Persian Empire Clashed with the Greeks

Darius wanted to expand the Persian territory. He first pushed the boundaries to include the Indus River valley. This includes parts of India and Pakistan. He also captured Egypt after a revolt. In Egypt, he oversaw the digging of a canal from the Nile River to the Red Sea. He also had a 10-foot (3.0-m) statue of himself built in Egypt. The Persian Empire controlled Egypt off and on for more than 130 years.

In 499 BCE, one of the satrapies in the empire started a rebellion. It was in Ionia, which was the area made up of Greeks living on the coast of western Turkey. Darius sent his army to put down the rebellion and restore peace. They eventually succeeded. But the Ionians were helped by the Greek city-states of Athens and Eretria.

After the Ionian rebellion ended, Darius wanted to punish the overseas Greeks. In 490 BCE, Darius sent one of his generals to do battle with the Greeks. The Persian

The modern-day Suez Canal connects the Mediterranean Sea to the Red Sea.

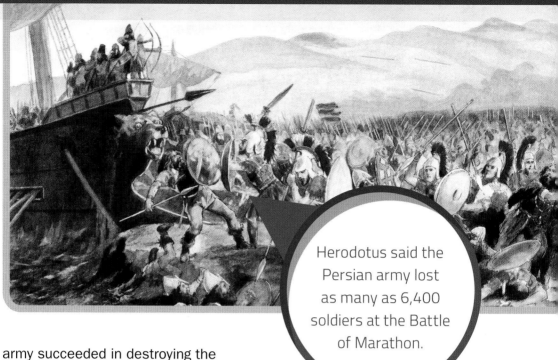

Herodotus said the Persian army lost as many as 6,400 soldiers at the Battle of Marathon.

army succeeded in destroying the city-state of Eretria. But the army was caught off-guard when a group of Athenian generals attacked them at Marathon. The Persian army suffered many losses and retreated to their ships waiting offshore. The Persian Empire would continue to do battle with the Greeks for many years.

THINK ABOUT IT

Before the Ionian rebellion, the Persian Empire had not done battle much with the Greeks. Why do you think it was important to Darius to destroy the overseas Greeks even after order was restored to Ionia?

5

Number of years the Ionian revolt against Persia lasted.

- Darius expanded the Persian Empire to the Indus River valley.
- His next re-conquest was Egypt, where he built a canal.
- A rebellion broke out in Ionia, and Greek city-states aided the Ionians.
- The Persian Empire wanted to punish the Greeks, but they did not always succeed.

School Prepared Boys to Be Soldiers

The Persians left little information about how children in the empire were educated. Most of what is written came from the Greek Herodotus. Historians are not sure which parts of his stories are accurate. But according to Herodotus, only boys went to school in ancient Persia. However, it wasn't a formal education. They spent their first years only with women. At age five they got to meet their father and begin their lessons. Most of their education taught them how to become good soldiers. They were taught how to shoot arrows. They learned how to ride horses. But the most important lesson was to always tell the truth. Lying was the worst offense.

Any Persian boy could receive this much education and become a soldier. But there was a big difference for royal sons. Writing on Darius's tomb showed that princes had to live up to royal expectations. They were supposed to have superior combat skills, such as throwing a spear both on foot and from horseback. They were also expected to be fair and just leaders. As teenagers, princes were assigned

Palace paintings of soldiers show how military skills were valued.

Art from the Persian Empire shows that a leader was supposed to make wise decisions.

to a group of four wise men. These teachers instructed them about four important qualities. The youth learned how to make wise decisions. They practiced justice in judging and punishing crimes. They also learned self-control, not only in these areas but in eating and drinking as well. If sent to war, they practiced the final trait, which was bravery in battle.

THINK ABOUT IT

School in the ancient Persian Empire was very different from schools in the United States today. Today's schools spend a lot of time teaching reading and writing. Physical education is only a small part of a student's day. What does this say about modern schools?

14

Age at which Persian royalty were assigned to a group of wise men for training.

- Only boys received an education in ancient Persia.
- Most of the lessons were on how to become a good soldier.
- Princes had lessons from four wise men.
- Princes were expected to have self-control and make wise decisions.

Royal Women Could Own Land

Historians and archaeologists still don't know much about what life was like for royal women who lived in ancient Persia. There are some documents from the Persian government that give insight called the Persepolis Fortification Tablets. However, many of the most common stories actually come from Herodotus and reflect Greek practices. A Persian king was all-powerful. However, his mother and his queen had the highest influence of all women at court. All other royal women were called princesses. Sometimes they were referred to as women of the palace. This included the king's other wives besides his queen.

Royal women were among the few people allowed to speak directly to the king. They often joined him for breakfast or dinner. The queen could be present when the king met with important people. She could also hold her own meetings. Royal women owned land and estates, which they could sell or rent. Some even had their own seal to approve business deals or payment to workers. They could help out family members in trouble by reducing punishment. They could also try to

6

Minimum number of wives Darius had.

- The queen and the king's mother ranked highest among royal women.
- Royal women could speak directly to the king.
- Royal women owned land and made business deals.
- The king gave female relatives in marriage to make alliances.

One well-known Persian queen is Esther, but there is no archaeological evidence that she existed.

save the life of a condemned person.

The king used his female relatives to make political alliances. Royal daughters were often given in marriage to foreign kings to assure a peace treaty or a land agreement.

Architecture and Jewelry Displayed Persian Art

Some of the best Persian art and architecture was at Persepolis. This was the grand capital city that Darius I founded in 518 BCE. The Apadana at Persepolis, which was used as a great meeting hall, was a good example. Columns at least 60 feet (18 m) high supported the roof. Huge double stairways showed a variety of reliefs. These were sculptures in which life-size carved figures were partly raised from the stone surfaces.

The gate at Persepolis

There are no women pictured in the building reliefs. But they were often found on small pieces of jewelry. Persians made jewelry out of gold or silver and decorated it with diamonds, emeralds, and other gemstones. Gold was also used in belt ornaments.

Animal carvings appeared on the open ends of bracelets. These might be the heads of lions, deer, or snakes. People were buried with their favorite jewelry. The jewelry and the reliefs were made by artists from all around the empire and reflected the many cultures.

150,000
Area, in square feet (13,935 sq m), of the Apadana at Persepolis.

- Persepolis was founded by Darius and had a large palace.
- Huge columns supported the roof of the palace's great hall.
- Women were pictured only on jewelry.
- Persians loved a variety of jewelry and were buried with it.

OTHER PALACE TREASURES

Darius also had a palace at Susa. Like Persepolis, it had many art treasures. Susa also had an Apadana. Its columns combined the building styles from many parts of the empire. A French team dug up Susa in the 1800s. Some artwork from the Susa palace is now displayed in museums in Paris.

Persian people also made bowls and other vessels out of gold.

Religion Was a Battle between Good and Evil

Historians think the prophet Zoroaster lived sometime between 1200 BCE and 600 BCE. He was called Zarathustra in the Persian Empire. He warned the people that earth was caught in a war between good and evil. The god of good was called Ahura Mazda. The god of

Zoroastrian temple built during the 500s BCE

5

Number of times fires were fed in Zoroastrian temples each day.

- The prophet Zoroaster warned Persians about the battle between good and evil.
- Those who chose good had to follow the three basic principles of good thoughts, good words, and good deeds.
- Fire was important to Persian religion.
- Persian kings considered themselves servants of Ahura Mazda.
- Priests were called magi.

evil was called Angra Mainyu. The people who followed Zoroastrianism believed in the idea of free will. The god of good and the god of evil were not all-powerful. Each person had to choose which side to follow. There were three basic principles for those who chose good. These were good thoughts, good words, and good deeds. Zoroastrians believed that all people would be judged after death. They would enjoy a happy afterlife if they had chosen goodness. Their afterlife would be miserable if they chose evil.

Zoroasters did not worship fire, but it was important to their religion. In Zoroastrian temples, an eternal flame was fed constantly to keep it burning. The Zoroastrians called Ahura Mazda their "wise lord." They believed that he created the earth. Persian kings saw themselves as Ahura Mazda's servants. They justified their claims to the throne and conquering more land because they believed they were protecting what Ahura Mazda had created. Kings still made sacrifices to other gods and goddesses, including those of captured peoples.

Priests were called magi. One of their jobs was to make sure Persian myths and traditions were passed on. The magi performed various rituals, which sometimes included dream interpretation. To get rid of evil omens, they often made sacrifices.

The Persian Military Was Feared but Not Unbeatable

Persian soldiers were armed for battle with spears, swords, bows and arrows, and sometimes axes. They had body armor made of metal scales stitched onto leather. They wore tunics and carried shields. The Persian navy was also a strong fighting force with its many warships. The ships were controlled by some of the best sailors from modern-day Lebanon.

Xerxes I used the Immortals against the Greeks at the Battle of Thermopylae in 480 BCE. The Immortals were Xerxes's special army. They were his best soldiers. He wanted revenge for losing the Battle of Marathon. He first demanded tributes from the city-states. Athens and Sparta refused. Xerxes led the Immortals

THE IMMORTALS

The Immortals were the 10,000 most highly trained soldiers in the Persian army. According to Herodotus, whenever one of them was sick, killed, or died, another soldier immediately took his place. There was never a time when there were fewer than 10,000 Immortals. It appeared that all the soldiers lived forever since there was never a gap when a soldier fell.

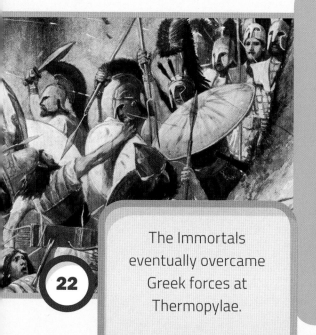

The Immortals eventually overcame Greek forces at Thermopylae.

into battle at the narrow pass at Thermopylae. The Greeks held out against the attack for several days. But they could not stop the Immortals. The Immortals marched over a mountain pass in the middle of the night. They sneaked in behind the Greek army and surprised them. The Greeks were surrounded. Some of the Greek soldiers retreated, but others stayed behind to fight to the death.

Xerxes used his army to take over more Greek city-states. His forces even attacked Athens. But many other Greek city-states decided to band together. Together Athens, Sparta, and many others gathered their warships and met the Persian navy at Salamis. The Greeks were greatly outnumbered but pulled off a victory. Historians are not sure how the battle went. Some think the number of Persian ships are to blame. As the Persian navy advanced on the Greeks, their boats may have become packed too closely together, making it hard to navigate.

1,000
Estimated number of warships Darius had.

- Soldiers used many weapons, including swords, spears, and bows and arrows.
- The Persian navy was a strong fighting force.
- Xerxes I used the Immortals against the Greeks at the Battle of Thermopylae.

Both the Persians and the Greeks had warships called *triremes*.

The Persian Empire Fell to Alexander the Great

After Xerxes I died in 465 BCE, Artaxerxes I came to the throne. He ruled for a long time. The Persian Empire was at peace during most of his reign. However, there were a few rebellions. Egypt broke away from the Persian Empire in 460 BCE. This rebellion lasted for six years.

Later, King Darius III became ruler of the Persian Empire. In 333 BCE, Darius and his army met the Macedonian conqueror named Alexander the Great. At the Battle of Issus, Alexander captured Darius's wife, his mother, and several of his children. Then in 331 BCE, King Darius faced off against Alexander

Tomb of Artaxerxes

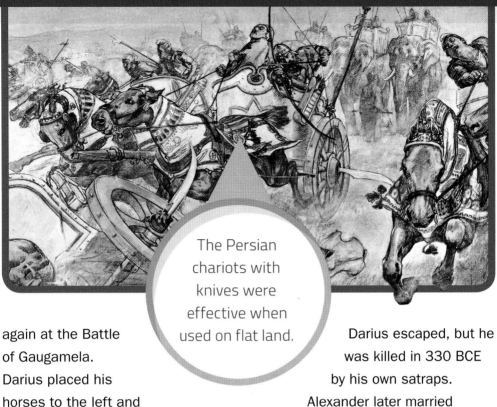

The Persian chariots with knives were effective when used on flat land.

again at the Battle of Gaugamela. Darius placed his horses to the left and right of his fighting forces. Mixed in with them were archers and soldiers on foot. At the front of the Persian line were 200 chariots that had sharp knives sticking out from the wheels. Historians have estimated Darius had more than 100,000 men. Despite Darius's greater numbers, Alexander made better use of his soldiers. They drew the Persians away from flat land, making the Persian horses and chariots less effective. A long struggle followed, but Alexander was victorious.

Darius escaped, but he was killed in 330 BCE by his own satraps. Alexander later married Stateira, one of Darius's daughters. As of 330 BCE, the Persian Empire was no more.

40
Number of years Artaxerxes I reigned.

- The Persian Empire was mostly at peace during the reign of Artaxerxes I.
- King Alexander of Macedonia captured some of Darius III's family at the Battle of Issus.
- The Persian Empire ended in 330 BCE.

Persia's Legacy Included Many Empires

After 330 BCE, Persia became part of Alexander the Great's empire. When Alexander died in 323 BCE, his empire was split apart. Three groups of people fought to build new empires in the Middle East.

The first were the Seleucids, who were related to one of Alexander's generals. They brought Macedonian and Greek culture with them. The Seleucids were overthrown by the Parthians. The Parthians were from

Artifacts from the city of Susa, which were made during the Seleucid Empire

northeastern Iran. Their empire lasted from 247 to 224 BCE. After the Parthians, the Sassanids came to power. The Sassanids were Persians. They were military rivals of the Roman Empire. During this time, Zoroastrianism became the official religion. None of these three groups was able to rule the entire area once controlled by the Persian Empire. But the Sassanian Empire lasted longer, from 224 BCE to 651 CE.

However, starting in the 630s CE, Arabs took over Persia. They brought with them a new religion called

636,296
Area, in square miles (1,647,999 sq km), of modern-day Iran.

- Three different groups fought to control ancient Persia after Alexander the Great died.
- Arab people began taking over Persian land in 630s CE and introduced the religion of Islam.
- Persia's name was changed to Iran in 1935, and its official religion is Islam.

Islam. In 1935, Persia's name was changed to Iran. An Islamic leader called Ayatollah Khomeini came to power in 1979. Today, Iran's official religion is Islam. Many of its government members are religious leaders.

Ayatollah Khomeini was first exiled from Iran in 1964 before returning in 1979 to take power.

12 Key Dates

1200–600 BCE
The prophet Zoroaster starts Zoroastrianism during this time period.

550 BCE
Cyrus the Great revolts against the Medes and starts the Persian Empire.

545–540 BCE
Cyrus conquers Lydia.

539 BCE
Cyrus overthrows King Nabonidus and adds Babylon to the Persian Empire.

530 BCE
Cyrus the Great is killed in battle; his son Cambyses takes control.

522 BCE
Darius I becomes king after Cambyses dies; he organizes the empire into 20 satrapies.

518 BCE
Darius founds the capital city of Persepolis.

499 BCE
The Ionian rebellion begins.

490 BCE
Darius's army invades Greece and is defeated at the Battle of Marathon.

480 BCE
After destroying Athens and winning the Battle of Thermopylae, Xerxes I loses to the Greek navy at Salamis.

465–425 BCE
Artaxerxes I reigns after Xerxes is killed.

331 BCE
Darius III is defeated by Alexander the Great at the Battle of Gaugamela; the Persian Empire is soon absorbed by Alexander.

Glossary

architecture
A style of building.

condemned
Sentenced to punishment.

couriers
People who carry messages for someone else.

culture
The ideas, customs, traditions, and way of life of a group of people.

dynasty
A series of rulers belonging to the same family.

legacy
Something handed down from one generation to another.

nomads
Members of a community who travel from place to place instead of living in the same place all the time.

seal
A design pressed into wax and made into a stamp. A seal is used to make a document official.

tribute
A kind of tax conquered people must pay the king.

For More Information

Books

Burgan, Michael. *Empires of Ancient Persia*. New York: Chelsea House, 2009.

Capek, Michael. *Understanding Iran Today.* Hockessin, DE: Mitchell Lane Publishers, 2014.

Hart, George. *Ancient Egypt*. New York: DK Publishing, 2014.

Visit 12StoryLibrary.com

Scan the code or use your school's login at **12StoryLibrary.com** for recent updates about this topic and a full digital version of this book. Enjoy free access to:

- Digital ebook
- Breaking news updates
- Live content feeds
- Videos, interactive maps, and graphics
- Additional web resources

Note to educators: Visit 12StoryLibrary.com/register to sign up for free premium website access. Enjoy live content plus a full digital version of every 12-Story Library book you own for every student at your school.

Index

About the Author

Peggy Caravantes is an award-winning author of over 25 middle-grade biographies and children's history books. She enjoys meeting her readers through school visits and tutoring.